Food Around the World

by Margie Burton, Cathy French, and Tammy Jones

People live all around
the world.

They like to eat many kinds of food.

Japan

I like to eat
a lot of fish.
Sometimes we
do not cook the fish.
We eat it raw
and put it in
some seaweed.
We eat rice, too.

4

Do you like to
eat vegetables? I do!
I eat my vegetables
with rice.

Korea

Vietnam

I like to
eat chicken
and vegetables
and rice noodles.
I like to put
some lime
on my food.

India

We like to eat fish.
We eat our fish
with rice. We
like to put
a hot, red sauce
on it.

Morocco

I like to eat pasta.
My pasta is so small
that it looks like rice.
I like to eat it with meat.

Ghana

Do you like my food? It is like bananas. I like to fry them when I eat them.

I like to
eat pancakes.
I like to
drink tea, too.

Argentina

I like to
eat meat that
comes from
my ranch. We
have some cows
on our ranch.

Mexico

I like to eat beans.
I eat my beans
in tortillas.
I like to put
hot peppers
into my food.

I like to
eat fish and
some foods
that we hunt
and kill. I
like to hunt
for food
with my dad.

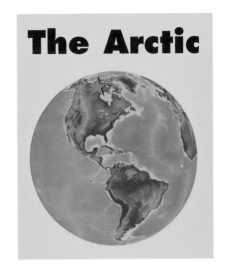

The Arctic

USA

Do you like
to eat my food?
I like to
eat pizza.
I make
my pizza
at home.

Here is how you can make pizza at home:

1. Get the things that you need for your pizza
   from the store.

2. These are the tools that you will need
   to make the pizza.

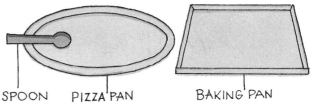

SPOON   PIZZA PAN   BAKING PAN

3. Open the pizza dough and pat
   it around in the pan.

4. Put some sauce on the dough and spread it around with a spoon.

5. Put the cheese on top of the pizza.

6. Bake the pizza at 450° for 12 to 15 minutes.